A GUIDED

The Awaking Wonder

EXPERIENCE

SALLY CLARKSON
with CLAY CLARKSON

BETHANYHOUSE
a division of Baker Publishing Group
Minneapolis, Minnesota

Contents

Introduction: Becoming a Wonder-full Mentor   5

1. Raising a Wonder-full Child   13

Section 1 FIRST LEARNING LENS: FOCUS ON HEART   21

2. Awaking Wonder through Faith   25

3. Awaking Wonder through Imagination   29

4. Awaking Wonder through Reading   33

5. Awaking Wonder through Story   37

6. Awaking Wonder through Talk   41

Section 2 SMART LEARNING LENS: FOCUS ON MIND   45

7. Awaking Wonder through Scripture   49

8. Awaking Wonder through Music   53

9. Awaking Wonder through Art   57

10. Awaking Wonder through wRiting   61

11. Awaking Wonder through Telling   65

Contents

Section 3 REACH LEARNING LENS: FOCUS ON STRENGTH   69

12. Awaking Wonder through Relationships   73

13. Awaking Wonder through Enjoyments   77

14. Awaking Wonder through Abilities   81

15. Awaking Wonder through Culture   85

16. Awaking Wonder through Home   89

Section 4 PLANNING: A TWELVE-MONTH PERSONAL PLANNER   93

Personal Planner: Making a Wonder-full Home Life   95

Twelve-Month Personal Planner   99

Notes   124

About the Authors   125

Introduction

Becoming a Wonder-full Mentor

Sally Clarkson

A local college hamburger joint is an unlikely place to transform the destiny of one woman. Yet I can still vividly picture the life-changing encounter even though it was over forty-five years ago.

My friend and I were sitting in a red vinyl booth, surrounded by black walls and dim lights. We sipped on Dr Peppers in red plastic cups while catching up on each other's lives. Our meetings took place weekly, sometimes at her apartment but often in this dark little diner. Becoming a Christian the year before in my tenth-floor college dorm room had started me on a journey of reading the Bible for the first time.

"Sally," she said softly, "I have been thinking about you and praying for you. I wanted to tell you I really believe that someday God is going to use you to change your world. You have such a clear and insightful grasp of Scripture, and I think many people in your lifetime will be encouraged by your messages. You have a way of seeing into people's hearts and encouraging them in the ways that they need it most. I just want you to know how much potential I see in your life. You are going to be a leader of many."

What she said to me in that brief moment of my young life filled my future with new possibilities. Her words lit a fire inside the deepest part of my heart that would lead me into a life of faith choices, risk taking, and reaching out for Christ. That fire has never died. Her trust in me made me want to believe in her. She spoke words that I had longed to hear—that my life mattered and that I had something of value to give to my world. Her generosity of friendship and mentoring spirit made me want to live up to her expectations of me.

This was my first personal experience with the power of mentoring and the impact one person can have upon another by intentionally choosing to encourage and inspire. My friend looked inside of me to unearth the potential she saw in my life; she then spoke those possibilities forward into my heart— what I might be, become, and do with the story of my life. She engaged me in her mentoring by caring about what I had to say. I believed what she taught me, not because of the content of her teaching but because of the person she saw in me. I believed in her because she believed in the person I could become.

Mentoring to Reach the Heart

A mentor wears several hats—life guide, coach, prophet, inspirer, teacher, and more. A mentor casts a vision into the heart and mind of the one they influence in order to point out and draw out the possibilities they see in that person. The mentor gives the other person vision and permission to become more than they are at that moment in time. A mentor is a catalyst.

As I look back on my growing-up years, I can see that my basic needs were met. I was fed, clothed, and cared for through those years. My schooling was average, but there was never a spark or love of learning or growing. Deep inside me there was a constant desire for something more, something I couldn't quite define. I carried in my mind confusing messages that I was either invisible and not that special to most people, or I was too much, even though I had many friends. I was not accustomed to anyone paying personal attention to me to look inside and see something of great value. My friend's words took me by surprise and filled me with hope.

On that day I felt seen. Someone thought my life had worth and value. My friend spoke forward into my life and encouraged me to believe that maybe I did have something special to pass on to others. Maybe I did have potential, and I had permission to imagine that my life could have a purpose in the grander scheme of things. She met my deep desire for meaning and purpose with the promise of possibilities.

During the year we met together, she taught me a great deal about the Bible and the Christian life. But after that particular meeting, my interest and enthusiasm for what she had to say became even more focused because she so personally cared for me. She had sparked my imagination for what I might do with my life—she created a sense of wonder in our time together of how God can use normal people to bring light and beauty to the world.

Perhaps this seems overly simplistic. Looking back on my life, I can see that God wired me to be the person I have become. However, it took a real-life person to unearth that possibility before I could see it for myself. It is what Jesus did for His disciples—He loved them, served them, spoke forward into their lives, and inspired them through His messages and actions. Mentoring is personal and given in relationship.

My husband, Clay, and I have written this book to encourage you in your journey of becoming a lifegiving mentor to your children. I wrote *Awaking Wonder*, and Clay wrote most of *The Awaking Wonder Experience*, but the concepts and principles you'll find come from both of us and from the wisdom and insights we have garnered together from over three decades as parents.

When you picture yourself as a mentoring parent—not just rehearsing and handing out facts and data, but sparking life and a love for learning and growing—you must consider how you are growing in your own life. Your children, who will be your followers, will be drawing out of the character you have cultivated in your own life. The influence you have on them will come directly from the maturity you display in relationships, how you handle responsibility, and how you live out your faith in Christ every day. You must be the kind of disciple you want them to become.

In other words, *becoming a worthy mentor will call you to become your best self in Christ*. Our desire in writing this planner is to help you become that kind of mentoring parent—to inspire you to become a godly model, to provide a simple structure for planning, and to help you write out your own creative thoughts and desires, focus on your own growth, and focus on your personal desires for your children. We hope this book will enable you to consider ways to awaken wonder for God in your family through the beauty of learning.

Cultivating Your Own Life as a Mentor

To keep this book simple, we've structured it around three main concepts, the learning lenses that will help you focus on awaking wonder in your child's heart, mind, and strength. However, the wonder-filled life that we want to help you create in your home is not just for your children, but also for you. It is your wonder-filled soul from which your children will draw life and inspiration.

In our daily worlds, it is so easy to focus on externals: how much money you make, what kind of position you have, what college you attended, your social status. But God asks us to focus on internals: what's in our hearts, who we follow, what motivates us, what we desire. Who we are on the inside will shape who we are on the outside.

An effective mentor influences from the overflow of a full mind and heart. What you value will be expressed in how you behave and relate to others. Whatever heart values you nurture—critical attitudes or love, fear or faith, judgment or grace, philosophy or wisdom, mediocrity or excellence—will be expressed in the choices and actions of your life. In other words, your heart will fuel your behavior.

Focus on Heart

The word *heart* is referenced in Scripture more than eight hundred times. God is concerned about our outward behavior, but when He looks at us He sees our inward person: "For God sees not as man sees, for man looks at the outward appearance, but the Lord looks at the heart" (1 Samuel 16:7). In the same way, if you want to have a lifelong influence on your children, you need to look not just at their childish behaviors, but also at their developing hearts. The wise mentor-parent knows that "as a face is reflected in water, so the heart reflects the real person" (Proverbs 27:19 NLT). To paraphrase a popular advertising slogan, "What happens in the heart stays in the heart." What happens in the heart will eventually create the real person. Consider ways you can focus on your own heart as a mentor:

- Examine your own heart by evaluating what you are storing and practicing there. Make personal goals to strengthen your heart.

- Are you storing up wisdom and faith from time you spend with God in Scripture and prayer? How can you turn what you are learning into how you are living?

- What unhealthy heart attitudes do you need to address— bitterness, criticism, fear, depression, despair, prejudice, hypocrisy? If you harbor these attitudes, then you will pass them on to your child. The bias of your heart will influence the way you teach.

- Do you ever resent the time your children take from you and the ways they deplete you emotionally, spiritually, and physically? Or do you feed the vision and passion of your heart that affirms the positive spiritual influence you can have on your children? Do you see that stewardship as a gift to your children and a profound way that you can worship and serve God?

- Jesus said that loving your neighbor as yourself is the heart of the Law (see Mark 12:31); that applies equally to loving your children. If *you* want to be loved unconditionally, given words of encouragement, and shown patience and grace, then that's what you should also give to your children. Unconditional love is the foundational influence that will ignite a child's heart to want to respond to you.

Focus on Mind

Jesus reminds us that obeying God starts with loving God, and one of the ways we are to do that is to "love the Lord your God . . . with all your mind" (Matthew 22:37). That means filling and shaping our minds with God's truth and wisdom. For your children, it means engaging their minds with the biblical ideas, truths, subjects, and stories that you want them to know and live by—asking questions, seeking opinions, guiding insights, and encouraging them to think, evaluate, ponder, imagine, and wonder. But to do that as a mentor-parent, you first must be loving God with *your* mind and strengthening *your* mental muscles.

- How are you intentionally filling your mind with good, true, and excellent knowledge? Evaluate the books you read, shows you watch, and websites you use (see Philippians 4:8). Whatever is feeding your ideals, ideas, and thoughts will shape your mind, so make it good and godly. As you think, so you will become (see Proverbs 23:7).

- If you want your children to grow intellectually, then you must invest in your own intellectual growth. I am challenged to read more widely because my children do—I am motivated to grow stronger in my own pursuit of knowledge so I can engage with what they are learning and thinking. The brain can keep learning for a lifetime.

- Choose three books to read in the next few months. Consider different genres: theology, fiction, biography, spiritual enrichment, science and creation, philosophy. Whatever you are reading, bring it into your teaching and discussions with your children.

- Just as attitudes of the heart are reflected in your behavior, so also will be the thoughts of your mind. Consider how to declutter your mind of repeated and distracting thoughts that can deplete your ability to offer wisdom, truth, and beauty. A disciplined thought life feeds a strong spiritual life. As Scripture says, "We are taking every thought captive to the obedience of Christ" (2 Corinthians 10:5).

Focus on Strength

Jesus affirmed that obedience—living in a way that will please the Lord—begins with several choices to "love the Lord your God" including "with all your strength" (Mark 12:30). The word He uses is not about physical strength, but about personal or spiritual strength—the force of one's being. In other words, we are to love God with everything that makes us who we are—wholeheartedly, no compromises, no competing loves, no conditions. We are all in, all the way, all the time. When our strength is directed toward God, we will grow stronger in character, integrity, and maturity because our lives will be aligned with the God who created us. When you are wholly aligned with the holy God and awakened to His wonder, there will be nothing between you and the wonder of God you want your children to know. A godly mentor-parent makes it a priority to stay personally and spiritually strong in Christ.

- Psalm 84 describes the worshiper "whose strength is in [God]" as going "from strength to strength" (vv. 5, 6). It is a picture of the follower who is continually trusting God and growing stronger in Him. Read Psalm 84 and use it to evaluate your own strength in the Lord. As a mentor, you will ask your children to be strong like you are.

- At the heart of growing strong is your will—are you willing to give your whole heart to following Christ? Will you exercise your spirit to become stronger every day—trusting God, learning from the Word, praying, understanding your strengths and weaknesses, growing in your gifts and skills, stepping out in faith? Your children are watching to see if your life with God is strong and genuine.

- Luke describes young Jesus as continuing to grow in "wisdom and stature, and in favor with God and men" (2:52). It's a good template to evaluate your personal growth as a mentor—are you growing stronger intellectually, physically, spiritually, and socially?

Mentoring is the way we chose to guide our children's learning and cultivate wonder and imagination throughout their years in our home. But taking that kind of personal interest in the overall development of your children is not easy—it comes with a cost. Being a faithful, godly mentor to them will require a commitment of your life and time—it will mean years of walking beside these disciples of Jesus you are shaping and influencing. As your children move from immaturity to maturity, you will need to exercise patience, faithfulness, and grace. As you grow older, you will need to keep your vision for your children in focus and your eyes on your goals as a mentoring parent. In all the challenges ahead, you will need to stay strong in Christ, always growing in character in order to become and remain a servant-leader to them through all the phases and seasons of life. It will be a life that will require sacrifices.

But on this side of that kind of life, we can say with confidence that it has been worth the sacrifices. As we consider our lives as parents, and the vision that God put in our hearts as a young couple, we can say that mentoring and discipling our four children is the best work we have accomplished with our lives. Our relationships with our adult children are the most fulfilling life relationships we could have desired.

Our hope and prayer is that you will be encouraged in your own vision for the wonder-filled journey of parenting, and for all that your children can become, as you work through this book to awaken wonder in their hearts, minds, and beings. The God of wonder is waiting to be with you on every step of your journey.

1

Raising a Wonder-full Child

Clay Clarkson

Sally and I both came to parenthood from traditional Christian homes and experiences—loving families, regular church attendance, twelve years of public school, state colleges. For us as children of the fifties and sixties, there were certainly speed bumps and potholes along the paths of our family journeys, but our parents did their best to raise us well. Nonetheless, by the time our daughter Sarah was born in 1984, we had moved on from our pasts and our parents' choices. We didn't know at that very early point in our parenting journey what to call our vision for family, but we knew we wanted to raise our children differently from how we had been raised. The picture had not yet come into clear focus for our future home life, but we were on a new and different path.

Even as we entered marriage in 1981, we agreed that we would want to raise our children to be more than just good Christian kids. We wanted them to be disciples of Jesus. After college, we both had joined the staff of an international Christian ministry dedicated to evangelism and discipleship.

That experience—of working to help fulfill the Great Commission of Jesus to go and "make disciples of all the nations" (see Matthew 28:18–20)—would profoundly shape our understanding of parenting. Later, as we talked and dreamed as new parents, we came to an inescapable conclusion: There was also a Great *Family* Commission, a call on our lives to make disciples of all our children. It was implied in Jesus' command, explicated in other Scriptures, and formed as a conviction in our spirits. We were being sent by God to a new mission field within the walls of our own home.

We knew what it meant to make disciples of adults, so we were already equipped and ready to apply the same discipleship principles that had shaped us to shaping our children. That was the easy part. Soon, though, we found ourselves faced with another inescapable conclusion: We could not disciple our children the way we envisioned by putting them in the school system. It was not a reaction, but simply a reality—we needed them to be at home with us. We didn't want to lose their hearts to classrooms, curriculums, peers, and activities that were not part of our home life for them. We didn't want their minds cluttered with unnecessary busywork or confused by beliefs and values that would not reflect our own. Discipleship meant a strategic relationship.

Mostly, though, our call was about parenting. We didn't want other adults influencing our children for over half their waking hours. We wanted to be the ones to shape their hearts and minds and to make them strong as the uniquely gifted and given people God would want them to become as His image bearers. We wanted their memories to be about our lifegiving home and table. We wanted them to live and learn at home, with us, and with God. We both knew that was the best gift we could give to our children as their parents for as long as we were able.

Thirty-five years later, with 20/20 hindsight, we can now give a name to the vision we sensed as new parents. We didn't have the words then, but now it's come into clear focus—it was all about awaking wonder. It was all about us wanting to be the ones who would awaken our children's hearts to the divinely designed beauty of life and learning. We wanted to be the ones to awaken their minds to the lifegiving grace and truth about

God that we had come to know and love and to awaken their spirits to the presence and reality of God in them, in our home, in our world, and in every corner of creation. We wanted to be the ones to bring light into their lives like Paul admonished believers to do:

> But all things become visible when they are exposed by the light, for everything that becomes visible is light. For this reason it says, "Awake, sleeper, and arise from the dead, and Christ will shine on you."
>
> Ephesians 5:13–14

That is the wonder that *Awaking Wonder* and this book, *The Awaking Wonder Experience*, are all about. It's not something that can be easily quantified or objectified, but it can be described and pursued. It's a mindset and a way of life that involves more than just a workbook and some assignments—it involves looking for and seeing opportunities every day to become a mentor and guide who can awaken your children to the wonder that is all around them. It is learning how to live awakened to the light of Christ shining on you as a family.

This guide is just that. It's not an educational handbook, a parenting manual, or a teaching curriculum. And though it provides resources for personal planning, it is not a comprehensive planner or plan. It is a "guided companion"—a kind of living and lifegiving map that will point you in the right direction. The insights, learning lenses, and suggestions in its chapters will direct you and your children onto and along the path of this thing we call the awaking wonder experience—discovering together the beauty of learning that comes from making everything visible in the light of Christ.

A guide can tell you where to go, but that information is helpful only if you can see where you're going. That's why this guide's chapters make use of another analogy—the lens. Think of corrective lenses. If you're nearsighted, you tend to see only what's right in front of you, and everything else is a blur. But corrective lenses enable you to see the rest of the world beyond your naturally limited field of vision—the lenses bring it all into focus. With them you can stop looking at your feet to make sure you aren't going to trip and start looking at the wonder of life that is ahead of you and all around you. Lenses help you see!

If you want to begin awaking wonder in your children, we provide some spiritual corrective lenses that will enable you to see more clearly all that you want your children to see. Getting life into focus that way begins, in this guide, with Jesus' response to a Jewish scribe's question: "Of all the commandments, which is the most important?" (Mark 12:28 NIV). Jesus brought the ultimate purpose and point of Scripture into clear focus:

> "The most important one," answered Jesus, "is this: 'Hear, O Israel: The Lord our God, the Lord is one. Love the Lord your God with all your heart and with all your soul and with all your mind and with all your strength.' The second is this: 'Love your neighbor as yourself.' There is no command-ment greater than these."
>
> vv. 29–31 NIV

Few caught the vision Jesus was casting at the time, but His summary of the Shema from Deuteronomy 6, the most important words of Scripture for Jews (see page 71), was the foundation upon which He would build His new church—not living by laws and rule keeping, but rather living for love and grace giving. As John the apostle would later say, "For the law was given through Moses; grace and truth came through Jesus Christ" (John 1:17 NIV). Love was the internal law, written on the heart by the Spirit of God, that would change the world. The Savior's answer to the curious scribe captured in a few words the very core of what would become the Christian mission. Here's the condensed version: Love God with all you are, and love people with all you're worth.

It's the first part of Jesus' answer, though, that provides the lenses for the chapters that will follow, which we hope will help you correct your vision for life with your children. It's about focusing on heart, mind, and strength. We've combined heart and soul, but the emphasis of Scripture is the same—a life that is awaking to the wonder of God begins with loving Him with your whole being. If any part of your being—heart, mind, or strength—is left out of the picture, then your vision will be out of focus. And that is true both for you and for your children.

Maybe you have the same kind of undefined vision for your children that we started with as parents. You know what you want your children to become and what you want your home life to be like, but you're just not sure what to call it. If so, perhaps awaking wonder can become the name of that longing in your heart as a parent. And we hope that the lenses we provide in *The Awaking Wonder Experience* can help you start to bring that vision for your family into focus. To that end, our hope is that this book will help you plan and make that journey as a mentoring parent with a wonder-full mission.

In the chapters that follow, you'll find three sections—one that focuses on heart, one on mind, and one on strength. Each section consists of five practical chapters, each containing a descriptive essay, suggested actions and activities, relevant Scripture passages, and two lined pages for ideas and resources (with suggestions to get you started and room to add your own). As you move at your own pace through those fifteen chapters, what you record in them will be a guidebook of lifegiving resources for your awaking wonder journey. When you begin filling out the Twelve-Month Personal Planner pages that conclude this book, those resources will become the daily directions you can use for that journey. As you follow the Holy Spirit's leading, you'll be on the path to awaking wonder.

Always keep in mind that there is no überplan, just *your* plan—the things *you* decide to do to awaken your child's heart, mind, and strength to the wonder of God's Word and work in the world. How you focus the learning lenses will be unique to your family. Think of what you do with this guide like making an itinerary for a long journey—your destination of awaking wonder will be the same as that of other parents taking the same trip, but the paths you take to get there will be different. You won't follow an itinerary made by someone else who doesn't know you or your children— the trip you make and take to awaking wonder will be yours alone.

Perhaps, though, you're thinking, *It's too late. I have the vision you're describing in my spirit, but it's too out of focus. I don't know where to start.* No matter where you are on the parenting journey—newbie, on the road, lost, veteran—it's never too late to make a fresh start! If God is in you, He is with you in your home and ready to work in the hearts and minds of your family to awaken them to the wonder of His reality and work in the world. It just takes a step forward.

The learning lenses in the rest of this book can help you get your family life in focus and find the awaking wonder experience that you long for with your children. Always keep in mind, though, that you don't have to do everything for every learning lens to begin that journey—anything you do is a step in the right direction. Awaking to the wonder of God's reality in life doesn't come all at once, but a little at a time, like light dawning on a new day.

As a Christian parent, you have been given new life in Christ, and He is waiting for you to awaken to that life so He can shine His light on you. That is the wonder He wants to awaken you to and what you are longing in your heart to awaken your children to. So try on the lenses that follow, and let them be the start for getting the vision for your family that is in your heart clear and focused. "Awake, sleeper, and arise from the dead, and Christ will shine on you" (Ephesians 5:14).

The Awaking Wonder Experience

This little book is a tool. There is no "best way," only your way. Whether you go page by page or flip and dip, it's not about finishing and ending, but starting and moving forward. Enjoy the journey.

- A good starting place is to read the introductory essay for each of the three main sections, which cover heart, mind, and strength.
- Wherever you are (it's all good), read the mini-essay for that chapter to orient to what that learning priority is about.
- Read the "Awaking Wonder at Home" ideas just to get started.
- Read the "Wonder-full Words of God" and ask Him to guide you.
- Start jotting down ideas that come to your spirit for things you can do (actions), say (words), and arrange (encounters).
- Jot down favorite resources you can use or resources you want to acquire.
- As you build up ideas and resources for the learning lenses, begin adding those to monthly pages in the Twelve-Month Personal Planner.
- Then just ask God to bless your wonder-full journey, and put your plans into action.

FIRST

LEARNING LENS

▼

Focus on Heart

FAITH
IMAGINATION
READING
STORY
TALK

FIRST
Learning Lens
Focus on Heart

We homeschooled each of our four children until they were ready to pursue more advanced learning away from home. When asked how we prepared them for college and beyond, we never say, "We educated them K–12, just like we were educated in school." Our model of learning at home was not based on cultural concepts of classrooms and curriculums. Rather, our vision for our children's learning was shaped by biblical concepts of discipleship and home. We called our model WholeHearted Learning, because our focus was first and always on preparing our children's hearts. We believed that if we wanted their minds to be prepared for life, it was necessary first to focus on their hearts. An immature heart could not produce a mature mind.

As our children made their way along their own living and learning journeys, the enduring and recurring question people asked us was always a variation of "Well, then, just how did you do that?" Even though we wrote a book about what we did, what can get lost in its pages are the non-negotiable and irreducible elements from which our entire learning model emerged. To shorten our answer to the question, we turned those elements into a simple acrostic that we called our FIRST learning priorities: Faith, Imagination, Reading, Story, and Talk. As we look back on all we did in our home, those five priorities are where we started in home education to make sure we kept our focus first on their hearts.

In our education-driven and curriculum-drenched culture, it is far too easy to think that age-graded studies and standardized testing are what should come first in learning. But aiming at the mind and missing the heart will not create a wholehearted child or young adult. Focusing on the world's standards of educational "success" can risk creating a child who might do well on tests of classroom learning but is unprepared for the tests of real life. That doesn't need to happen.

This section will help you think about how to focus on the FIRST learning priorities in order to awaken a sense of wonder in your child's heart for a God who is infinitely knowable. You are giving them reasons and a vision for why to learn more about God, their Creator, and the wonder-filled life He has made for us to enjoy.

It cannot be said too strongly that the most important influence on your child's heart will be . . . you. If you want to awaken wonder in your child's heart, then you first must awaken it in your own. They will learn what it means to live with an awakened wonder for life and learning because they see it in you first. So, start this wonder-filled adventure by applying the FIRST learning priorities to your own heart.

Focusing My Life

As a mentor to my child, how am I focusing on developing my own heart? What am I doing to awaken wonder for God in my own spiritual life?

_____

_____

_____

_____

2

Awaking Wonder through
FAITH

Most adult believers have made peace with their own faith. But for many Christian parents, that may not always be the case when it comes to their *child's* faith. For some, that faith is "not ready for prime time" and can be casually dismissed; for others it is a fully formed faith and must be treated that way. Jesus didn't see a child's faith as either, yet He made clear that childhood faith is real and growing when He warned His disciples that "if anyone causes one of these little ones *who believe in me* to sin" (Matthew 18:6 NET, emphasis added), they might as well be thrown into the sea to drown. Jesus clearly affirmed the spiritual nature of young children—that they could believe, or have faith, in Him. And just as important, He affirmed that a parent should be very careful not to do anything that could cause their child to "sin," or to "stumble," in their faith.

It is significant that faith is the first of the FIRST learning priorities. Awaking wonder in your child's heart must begin with a clear and unequivocal understanding that their developing faith, even though not yet mature, is still every bit as real and true to them as yours is to you. In fact, a child's unadulterated (literally) sense of belief and wonder is something to be cultivated and protected like a growing plant.

Awaking wonder in your child will not happen just by your doing and saying "wonder-full" things. Those are important, and this book will help you think through what they can be. But in order to fully awaken your child to the wonder of this life, all of that must be focused through faith. That's where an awaking wonder begins—in the reality and realization that a wonderful God is alive in our lives every day. Only a heart enlivened by faith can be awake to the wonders of life.

Awaking Wonder at Home with Faith

- Your children's faith expressions will not always be fully formed. Learn to listen for "faith words" in their casual conversation— "I think God . . ." or "I'm going to pray . . ." or "I read in the Bible . . ." Take time to ask questions and talk about the faith behind their words.

- Family prayer can be a kind of faith incubator and instigator. When you are acknowledging that you believe God is real and listening to you, it gives your children the opportunity to consider what that means for their own prayers. Your faith will stir up their faith.

- How you respond to difficulties, trials, and afflictions in your family can be a powerful example of faith for your children. It will take a lifetime to develop a mature and faithful response to hard times, but it begins for your child by seeing it done at home and in your life.

Wonder-full Words of God about Faith

"And whoever welcomes a little child like this in my name welcomes me. But if anyone causes one of these little ones who believe in me to sin, it would be better for him to have a large millstone hung around his neck and to be drowned in the depths of the sea."

Matthew 18:5–6 NIV1984

"Do not let your hearts be troubled. Trust in God; trust also in me. In my Father's house are many rooms; if it were not so, I would have told you. I am going there to prepare a place for you."

John 14:1–2 NIV1984

Trust in the Lord with all your heart and do not lean on your own understanding. In all your ways acknowledge him, and he will make your paths straight.

Proverbs 3:5–6

And without faith it is impossible to please God, because anyone who comes to him must believe that he exists and that he rewards those who earnestly seek him.

Hebrews 11:6 NIV

Wonder-full Ideas for Faith

ACTIONS—What I can do

☐ _____

☐ _____

☐ _____

☐ _____

☐ _____

☐ _____

WORDS—What I can say

☐ _____

☐ _____

☐ _____

☐ _____

☐ _____

☐ _____

ENCOUNTERS—What I can arrange

☐ _____

☐ _____

☐ _____

☐ _____

☐ _____

☐ _____

RESOURCES—What I can acquire or provide

☐ *Our 24 Family Ways: A Family Devotional Guide* by Clay Clarkson

☐ *The Lifegiving Parent* by Clay and Sally Clarkson

☐ *Own Your Life* by Sally Clarkson

☐ _____

☐ _____

☐ _____

3

Awaking Wonder through
IMAGINATION

Perhaps you're thinking, *What does imagination have to do with my child's heart? It's just a childhood phase.* But think again. And think bigger. All of creation is an expression of the perfect imagination of God. Genesis chapter one shows God imagining the world He wants to create, and then making it. Arguably, we share that quality of His nature in the divine image that we carry. As *sub-creators* (from J.R.R. Tolkien), we are "little makers" who use our God-imaged imagination as stewards of this creation and are charged with the divine mission to "subdue" the earth and "rule over it." God imagined us imagining how we could do that.

But there's more to imagination than that. Our capacity to imagine is our ability to see things in our mind that may or may not exist in the material, or immaterial, world around us. If that sounds like faith, that's no accident. Imagination is the mental faculty that enables us to believe in a personal God whom we cannot touch, a heavenly realm that we cannot see, a divine kingdom that is both now and not yet. Imagination enables us to believe in a Savior who died and rose again for us.

So it's no wonder that imagination is so critical to awaking wonder in your child. It is the key that unlocks the door of the heart to belief in

Christ, which brings with it the transforming Spirit of God. Paul says it is "with your heart that you believe and are justified" (Romans 10:10 NIV). He also prays that "the eyes of your heart may be enlightened" so you can know all that God has done for you in eternity (Ephesians 1:18). All the wonders of God's grace and mercy will be known by your child only through a redeemed imagination. When you cultivate, feed, and form the imaginations of your children, you awaken wonder in their hearts.

Awaking Wonder at Home with Imagination

- Don't be afraid of your child's imagination. Like any other neutral mental faculty, it just needs to be directed and fed the right things. And like a muscle, it needs to be strengthened if it is going to be brought into the service of saving belief in Christ.
- A simple way to exercise the imagination when you're together as a family is with an "imagination train." Start telling a story—fable, fantasy, fairy tale—then steer the story to someone else, and so on. Each person has to keep the story moving forward to a conclusion.
- Imagination needs good food to keep it growing. For that there is no substitute for a home library (on bookshelves, not on a device) filled with stories of all kinds, interesting books of information and history, poetry, art, and all things of printed page.

Wonder-full Words of God about Imagination

I pray also that the eyes of your heart may be enlightened in order that you may know the hope to which he has called you, the riches of his glorious inheritance in the saints, and his incomparably great power for us who believe.

Ephesians 1:18–19 NIV1984

Now faith is being sure of what we hope for and certain of what we do not see.

Hebrews 11:1 NIV1984

For it is with your heart that you believe and are justified, and it is with your mouth that you confess and are saved. As the Scripture says, "Anyone who trusts in him will never be put to shame."

Romans 10:10–11 NIV1984

"The seed is the word of God. Those along the path are the ones who hear, and then the devil comes and takes away the word from their hearts, so that they may not believe and be saved."

Luke 8:11–12 NIV

Wonder-full Ideas for Imagination

ACTIONS—What I can do

- ☐ _____
- ☐ _____
- ☐ _____
- ☐ _____
- ☐ _____
- ☐ _____

WORDS—What I can say

- ☐ _____
- ☐ _____
- ☐ _____
- ☐ _____
- ☐ _____
- ☐ _____

ENCOUNTERS—What I can arrange

- ☐ _____
- ☐ _____
- ☐ _____
- ☐ _____
- ☐ _____
- ☐ _____

RESOURCES—What I can acquire or provide

- ☐ *The Lifegiving Home* by Sally and Sarah Clarkson
- ☐ *The Lifegiving Parent* by Clay and Sally Clarkson, chapter 9
- ☐ _____
- ☐ _____
- ☐ _____
- ☐ _____

4

Awaking Wonder through

READING

The Bible is not just a necessary accessory to faith, a practical supplement added as a way to keep written records of the long story of God's work in this world. From the beginning, God designed us to be people of the written word because that is how He always intended to reveal himself to us. Paul reminds Timothy that "all Scripture is inspired by God" (2 Timothy 3:16). Every word of the holy writings is useful to us because it is part of the God-breathed Word. He is the Word of words.

Your children enter this world ready to read. You don't really teach them how to read—that ability is already hardwired into their brains. You simply direct and release their God-designed capability for reading. That capacity for language, but especially for reading, will determine everything that goes into their hearts to shape who and what they will become—their beliefs, values, character, virtues, loves, purposes, drives, vocations, and more. Reading is feeding a life.

Sarah, our oldest child, wrote *Read for the Heart*, a book-length feast of the point that this one-page nibble attempts to make. She said: "Every book I've read and every story that has made itself a part of my imagination has taught me something about what it means to live life well. I'm passionate about reading because I'm passionate about life."[1] Sarah's wonder for life was awakened by reading and by books.

One of the most heart-shaping things you can do for your children that will awaken them to the wonders of God and life is to cultivate in them a love for reading. Give them the best books, read books aloud together, delight in the beauty and power of written words. You will awaken wonder and the ability to be self-awakened to wonder.

Awaking Wonder at Home with Reading

- Well-read is well fed. In the same way your child's body needs good food to grow, your child's heart needs good books and reading. "Junk food" reading will not grow a strong heart. Be intentional about cultivating an appetite for reading well.

- Read aloud. Get the family together for an evening on the couch and read a favorite book out loud. Both eyes and ears can be trained to "read" well. Reading aloud strengthens attention, retention, and more. And it's a powerful and positive reading experience.

- Ownership builds readership. If you build a personal library, your children will come, and they will read. Give them a nice bookcase and begin to fill its shelves with good reading. Give them a small fund they can use to buy good books. Reading happens!

Wonder-full Words of God about Reading

All Scripture is God-breathed and is useful for teaching, rebuking, correcting and training in righteousness, so that the servant of God may be thoroughly equipped for every good work.

2 Timothy 3:16–17 NIV

For the word of God is alive and active. Sharper than any double-edged sword, it penetrates even to dividing soul and spirit, joints and marrow; it judges the thoughts and attitudes of the heart.

Hebrews 4:12 NIV

Jesus did many other things as well. If every one of them were written down, I suppose that even the whole world would not have room for the books that would be written.

John 21:25 NIV

Love the Lord your God with all your heart and with all your soul and with all your strength. These commandments that I give you today are to be on your hearts. Impress them on your children.

Deuteronomy 6:5–7 NIV

Wonder-full Ideas for Reading

ACTIONS—What I can do

- ☐ _____
- ☐ _____
- ☐ _____
- ☐ _____
- ☐ _____
- ☐ _____

WORDS—What I can say

- ☐ _____
- ☐ _____
- ☐ _____
- ☐ _____
- ☐ _____
- ☐ _____

ENCOUNTERS—What I can arrange

☐ _____

☐ _____

☐ _____

☐ _____

☐ _____

☐ _____

RESOURCES—What I can acquire or provide

☐ *Read for the Heart* by Sarah Clarkson

☐ *Educating the WholeHearted Child* by Clay and Sally Clarkson, chapter 12

☐ *Classics to Read Aloud to Your Children* by William F. Russell

☐ _____

☐ _____

☐ _____

5

Awaking Wonder through STORY

Story is the heartbeat of life. If there is no story, it's the same as saying there is no life. Without story, we are just accidents of impersonal nature caught up in, well, just existence. There is no wonder in that sad reality. Your parental determination must be to awaken your child's heart to the wonder of the story he is caught up in living—his story, your family's story, your legacies, and how they are all part of God's larger stories of redemption and the kingdom. As you awaken your child's heart to the wonder of story, you awaken him to life.

It is said that "if you want someone to know the truth, tell them. If you want them to love the truth, tell them a story."[1] Story gives the facts of truth that we put in their heads a place to come alive in their hearts with the stories of truth. Story gives your child a way to understand that mountains can be climbed, dragons defeated, battles won, and quests completed.

Sarah, who envisioned and started the Storyformed website, wrote: "A story-formed imagination is naturally driven to real-world action. The great point of excellent stories is to wake us up to beauty, dress down our pride, and teach us how to live with courage, compassion, and creativity."[2] Stories awaken your child to the wonders of all that is good, true, and beautiful. Story shows us what can be.

We talk about creating a storyformed life for our children—a life shaped and sharpened by the power of story. But even more important is a story-formed heart—a heart that is fully awakened to the wonder of the story that God is telling and their place in that story. Awaken your child's heart to the wonder of life through story.

Awaking Wonder at Home with Story

- Children (of all ages) love a good story. Reading THE CHRONICLES OF NARNIA series by C. S. Lewis is a perfect way to use story to capture imaginations and also discover spiritual truths in allegory, symbols, and analogies. Narnia storifies life, helping us tell our own stories.

- Jesus was a masterful storyteller. The truths He told in sermons were just as clear and perhaps more memorable when told using stories. Regularly read and discuss Jesus' parables. Also use a good Bible storybook to remember the many stories of Scripture.

- Look for other story formats. Poetry, the most complex form of the English language, allows stories to be told in beautiful words that make the story come alive. Fables tell stories with animals and in ways that make the lessons memorable and meaningful.

Wonder-full Words of God about Story

In the beginning God created the heavens and the earth. Now the earth was formless and empty, darkness was over the surface of the deep, and the Spirit of God was hovering over the waters.

Genesis 1:1–2 NIV

Then Jesus was led up by the Spirit into the wilderness to be tempted by the devil. And after He had fasted forty days and forty nights, He then became hungry. And the tempter came. . . .

Matthew 4:1–2 (Read the rest of the story in vv. 3–11.)

And He said, "A man had two sons. The younger of them said to his father, 'Father, give me the share of the estate that falls to me.' So he divided his wealth between them. . . ."

Luke 15:11–12 (Read the rest of the story in vv. 13–32.)

For He rescued us from the domain of darkness, and transferred us to the kingdom of His beloved Son, in whom we have redemption, the forgiveness of sins.

Colossians 1:13–14

Wonder-full Ideas for Story

ACTIONS—What I can do

☐ _____

☐ _____

☐ _____

☐ _____

☐ _____

☐ _____

WORDS—What I can say

☐ _____

☐ _____

☐ _____

☐ _____

☐ _____

☐ _____

ENCOUNTERS—What I can arrange

- ☐ _____
- ☐ _____
- ☐ _____
- ☐ _____
- ☐ _____
- ☐ _____

RESOURCES—What I can acquire or provide

- ☐ *Caught Up in a Story* by Sarah Clarkson
- ☐ *The Jesus Storybook Bible* by Sally Lloyd-Jones, illustrated by Jago
- ☐ THE CHRONICLES OF NARNIA series by C. S. Lewis
- ☐ _____
- ☐ _____
- ☐ _____

6

Awaking Wonder through
TALK

What was your secret for parenting? What did you do?" Whenever we get those questions, we're always insistent that it was all by faith and grace and that we had no divine formula for biblical parenting. And yet, one element of influence connected everything we did like a long gold thread—spoken words. We did all we could to create and sustain a verbal atmosphere in our home for our children.

When Jesus told the parable of the sower, the seed being sown was the Word of God. We all try to sow God's Word! However, it was only when the seed fell in good soil that it would take root, grow, and produce an abundant crop. So the real question should be, "How do I create good soil to grow good children?" What we found is that good soil cannot be formed apart from a verbal atmosphere in the home.

But the Logos, or the Word, of God is not just propositional truth and information mediated to us through prophets onto paper to feed to our children. God's Logos was incarnated for us in the person of Jesus Christ, and His truth was delivered verbally and personally. In the same way, you will embody God's truth for your children to be given verbally and personally. They will see and hear the Logos alive in you.

Creating a verbal atmosphere at home is arguably the most important yet least used priority for awaking wonder in children. In our busy, fragmented, screen-ified culture, we talk as families for only minutes each day. A heart deprived of conversation, words, and ideas will be an uncultivated heart. A heart cultivated with words will be good soil. Wonder for God and His creation can be awakened through shared vocabulary, language, and ideas. Talk about it!

Awaking Wonder at Home with Talk

- There is no better place to talk as a family than at the table, so if you're not eating a meal together each day, start. Then, have conversation starters on hand, and be prepared to engage in discussions about personal stories and current events. Be creative.
- Set aside time each week for family discussions. Let everyone know the topic—Scripture, current events, history, best food, whatever. Ask everyone to come ready to talk about, debate, and discuss the topic. This is a lighthearted time to get everyone talking.
- Learn the art of asking good questions that are simple, short, strategic, sweet, and stimulating. They should be open questions seeking opinions, feelings, information, or analysis. The purpose of good questions is to stimulate good conversation and interaction.

Wonder-full Words of God about Talk

Let the message of Christ dwell among you richly as you teach and admonish one another with all wisdom through psalms, hymns, and songs from the Spirit, singing to God with gratitude in your hearts.

Colossians 3:16 NIV

Be wise in the way you act toward outsiders; make the most of every opportunity. Let your conversation be always full of grace, seasoned with salt, so that you may know how to answer everyone.

Colossians 4:5–6 NIV

But in your hearts revere Christ as Lord. Always be prepared to give an answer to everyone who asks you to give the reason for the hope that you have. But do this with gentleness and respect.

1 Peter 3:15 NIV

Do not let any unwholesome talk come out of your mouths, but only what is helpful for building others up according to their needs, that it may benefit those who listen.

Ephesians 4:29 NIV

Wonder-full Ideas for Talk

ACTIONS—What I can do

- ☐ _____
- ☐ _____
- ☐ _____
- ☐ _____
- ☐ _____
- ☐ _____

WORDS—What I can say

- ☐ _____
- ☐ _____
- ☐ _____
- ☐ _____
- ☐ _____
- ☐ _____

ENCOUNTERS—What I can arrange

- ☐ _____
- ☐ _____
- ☐ _____
- ☐ _____
- ☐ _____
- ☐ _____

RESOURCES—What I can acquire or provide

- ☐ *The Lifegiving Table* by Sally Clarkson
- ☐ *The Lifegiving Parent* by Clay and Sally Clarkson
- ☐ *Every Moment Holy* by Douglas McKelvey
- ☐ _____
- ☐ _____
- ☐ _____

Section 2

SMART

LEARNING LENS

▼

Focus on Mind

SCRIPTURE
MUSIC
ART
wRITING
TELLING

SMART
Learning Lens
Focus on Mind

There's more to the mind than meets the "I know." The accumulation of knowledge is a part of mental development to be sure, but your child's mind is more than just a cellular repository of facts, information, and cultural trivia. Data and details alone will never awaken wonder in your child's mind and actually might put your child to sleep!

If asked about a child's mind, many would simply talk about the function of the brain as a physical, bodily organ. But Scripture sees the mind as more—as part of our immaterial nature. In 1 Corinthians, Paul talks about the "spiritual man" (2:15 TLB) and then quotes Isaiah 40:13, "For who has known the mind of the Lord that he will instruct Him?" (1 Corinthians 2:16). Though God exists without physical form, Paul uses the same word for God's mind (*nous*) that he uses for his own mind (see 14:14), and then he says, "But we have the mind [*nous*] of Christ" (2:16). The immaterial workings of Christ's mind become part of our own minds.

Jesus declared the greatest commandment in the Law to be "love the Lord your God with all your heart and with all your soul and *with all your mind*" (Matthew 22:37 NIV, emphasis added). *Mind* wasn't in the Old Testament passage Jesus quoted (see Deuteronomy 6:5), but it was in His mind. The term He uses (a form of *nous*) can also be translated *imagination*—the ability to conceive things that exist apart from our physical experience. In other words, mind is more than the brain.

Paul commands us in Romans 12:2 to "be transformed by the renewing of your mind" so that we can see and show all that is good about God. To be transformed means to change from one thing into something new, much like two images that are morphed together. Awaking wonder, then, must start there—changing who we are by changing how we think. In Ephesians, Paul describes that as a spiritual process, one of being "renewed in the spirit of your mind" (4:23).

When you focus on the five SMART learning priorities of this chapter—Scripture, Music, Art, wRiting, Telling—you will be growing a mind. Your goal is not just to fill your child's mind with facts and information but to renew her mind spiritually. With these five priorities, you are focusing on mental food that will grow a strong mind. A smart mind.

But there is a catch. If you want to see that happen in your child's mind, you need to be SMART about growing and renewing your own mind. How are you feeding your mind so that it keeps growing? What books are you reading? What music is filling and shaping your mind? What art do you enjoy and make? What are you writing from your renewed mind? Be smart! Not just for your children, but for you.

Focusing My Life

As a mentor to my child, how am I focusing on my own mind? What am I doing to awaken wonder for God in my own mental life?

7

Awaking Wonder through SCRIPTURE

A few years ago, the Christian Booksellers Association offered the slogan, "What goes into the mind comes out in a life." As a parent you don't need a slogan to know that whatever goes into your children's minds feeds who they are becoming. That's why you also instinctively know that all of Scripture—verses, stories, truths, principles, parables, analogies—is the most important mind food for your children's lives. In the same way that they need living foods for their bodies, they also need living food for their spirits. Hebrews 4:12 says that "the word of God is alive and active" (NIV). Scripture is living food for your children's growing minds.

But there's the other side of the slogan too. Paul commanded us not to be "conformed" to the world's way of thinking (see Romans 12:2). It is just as easy for a mind to be shaped by the world as it is by the Word. However, rather than being overly fearful, our best parental defense against the world's words is to mount a strong biblical offense with God's words. Paul reminds Timothy that "all Scripture is God-breathed" and works to create a godly servant who is "equipped for every good work" (see 2 Timothy 3:16–17). Start with Scripture.

"The unfolding of your words gives light; it gives understanding to the simple" (Psalm 119:130 NIV). In other words, as your child is learning how to learn, Scripture helps him learn what it means to be a good and godly person. Scripture is like a lamp that can give your child's mind the light he needs to stay on God's path of life (see Psalm 119:105). But Jesus made clear at the end of His Sermon on the Mount that this kind of mind- and life-shaping wisdom comes only to the one who hears His words and "puts them into practice" (Matthew 7:24 NIV). His words come out in a life.

Awaking Wonder at Home with Scripture

- The best way to begin to shape your children's minds with Scripture is by having a daily family devotional time. There is no biblical directive for how to do that, so find whatever time of day, place, and pattern work best for your own family. Start the habit early.
- If you want Scripture in your children's minds, engage them in age-appropriate discussion about God's Word. One easy way to get them thinking and talking is to read a Scripture and ask, "What do you think God wants us to know, be, do, or believe in this passage?"
- Our Family Devotional ARTS is a quick outline for a "just add Bible" family devotion: (1) Ask a question (something fun and interactive); (2) Read the Bible (out loud, with expression); (3) Talk about it (what it says and means); and (4) Speak to God (pray together to apply it).

Wonder-full Words of God about Scripture

All Scripture is God-breathed and is useful for teaching, rebuking, correcting and training in righteousness, so that the servant of God may be thoroughly equipped for every good work.

2 Timothy 3:16–17 NIV

And do not be conformed to this world, but be transformed by the renewing of your mind, so that you may prove what the will of God is, that which is good and acceptable and perfect.

Romans 12:2

For the word of God is alive and active. Sharper than any double-edged sword, it penetrates even to dividing soul and spirit, joints and marrow; it judges the thoughts and attitudes of the heart.

Hebrews 4:12 NIV

How can a young person stay on the path of purity? By living according to your word.

Psalm 119:9 NIV

As for God, his way is perfect: The Lord's word is flawless; he shields all who take refuge in him.

Psalm 18:30 NIV

Wonder-full Ideas for Scripture

ACTIONS—What I can do

☐ _____

☐ _____

☐ _____

☐ _____

☐ _____

☐ _____

WORDS—What I can say

☐ _____

☐ _____

☐ _____

☐ _____

☐ _____

☐ _____

ENCOUNTERS—What I can arrange

☐ _____

☐ _____

☐ _____

☐ _____

☐ _____

☐ _____

RESOURCES—What I can acquire or provide

☐ *Our 24 Family Ways: A Family Devotional Guide* by Clay Clarkson

☐ *The Action Bible* by Sergio Cariello, illustrator, and Doug Mauss, editor

☐ *Praying the Scriptures for Your Children* by Jodie Berndt

☐ _____

☐ _____

☐ _____

8

Awaking Wonder through
MUSIC

Music is part of our life with God, a universal experience that is found throughout the Scriptures—we sing, angels sing, Jesus sings, stars sing, all creation sings, heavenly beings sing, and even God sings. But even more important, music is a fundamental language for our praise and worship of God. You cannot fully worship God without "singing and making melody with your heart to the Lord" (Ephesians 5:19). Arguably, God has made us with music in our souls for that ultimate spiritual purpose—to worship Him in song, now and in eternity.

Music is part of our human nature, but neuroscience has found it is also an important part of brain development—language and melody are processed in the same part of the brain; children exposed to music before age seven show greater brain development; music stimulates regions of the brain that process positive emotions. When you consider the ways that music is so intimately tied to the *brain* as an organ, it is not difficult to make the connection to the *mind* as a spiritual reality. In a final command about how to live as Christ's body, Paul tells the Colossian church to wisely teach and admonish one another with music, by "singing with thankfulness in your hearts" (Colossians 3:16). Music would touch the inmost part of their being. For believers who shared the mind of Christ, music was to be a nonnegotiable part of their lives.

You can also respond to this verse as a family, which is a microcosm of the body of Christ. You can make music a critical part of wisely awaking your child's mind—their spiritual nature—to the wonder of all that God intends for us as His creatures. Like the muses of the arts in Greek mythology, let music inspire your child's mind with wonder.

Awaking Wonder at Home with Music

- Introduce your children, beginning at early ages, to quality instrumental music that elicits positive emotions. We enjoyed baroque classical music; piano, violin, acoustic guitar, and hammered dulcimer music; show tunes; and movie soundtracks.
- Make listening to and singing hymns, psalms, and spiritual songs a part of your daily musical diet. Whether the music is traditional or contemporary, the wisdom of the words will come through. We enjoyed the music of Fernando Ortega, Celtic hymns, and others.
- Introduce your children to musical instruments that create melody and can encourage singing, such as piano, violin, ukulele, and others. Help them choose and learn all kinds of songs, but especially spiritual songs. Encourage them to try writing their own songs.

Wonder-full Words of God about Music

Let the word of Christ richly dwell within you, with all wisdom teaching and admonishing one another with psalms and hymns and spiritual songs, singing with thankfulness in your hearts to God.

Colossians 3:16

And do not get drunk with wine, for that is dissipation, but be filled with the Spirit, speaking to one another in psalms and hymns and spiritual songs, singing and making melody with your heart to the Lord.

Ephesians 5:18–19

He put a new song in my mouth, a song of praise to our God; many will see and fear and will trust in the Lord.

Psalm 40:3

My heart is steadfast, O God, my heart is steadfast; I will sing, yes, I will sing praises! Awake, my glory! Awake, harp and lyre! I will awaken the dawn. I will give thanks to You, O Lord, among the peoples; I will sing praises to You among the nations. For Your lovingkindness is great to the heavens and Your truth to the clouds.

Psalm 57:7–10

Wonder-full Ideas for Music

ACTIONS—What I can do

☐ _____

☐ _____

☐ _____

☐ _____

☐ _____

☐ _____

WORDS—What I can say

☐ _____

☐ _____

☐ _____

☐ _____

☐ _____

☐ _____

ENCOUNTERS—What I can arrange

☐ _____

☐ _____

☐ _____

☐ _____

☐ _____

☐ _____

RESOURCES—What I can acquire or provide

☐ *Hymns for the Lifegiving Home* by Joel Clarkson

☐ *Midwinter Carols* by Joel Clarkson

☐ *Spiritual Lives of the Great Composers* by Patrick Kavanaugh

☐ _____

☐ _____

☐ _____

9

Awaking Wonder through
ART

A rt is visual language. Every artist expresses something in their art-work—an idea, image, vision, beauty, mystery, concept, feeling, philosophy, delight. They are painting, sculpting, sketching, making, or putting into some physical form what they alone see in their minds. Rather than words, they use lines, colors, shapes, shades, composition, perspective, and more. Rather than verbally, their art speaks visually.

In the same way we studied language arts skills for speaking and writing with our children, we also studied visual arts skills. In an increasingly visual and nonverbal modern culture, we wanted to equip them to show as well as to tell, to illustrate as well as explicate, what is in their minds. Our goal was not to make them artists, but simply to give them the ability to draw and use color in the same way that they speak and use words. The mind sees before it says, and art is the language for putting into visual "words" what it sees, feels, and imagines.

Art exercises the imagination, showing what the mind sees. Beginning with God creating out of nothing in Genesis, art shows up throughout Scripture to give physical form to spiritual realities, to express beauty, and to glorify God. One way to awaken your child's mind to God's wonder is through appreciating the work of gifted artists of all kinds—to "hear" and engage with what they are saying in their artwork. Just enjoying the beauty of art is an act of awaking wonder all its own. But don't let the absence of artistic gifts prevent you and your children from learning your own artistic language. Observing, drawing, and coloring can help awaken the mind of your children to the wonder that God, the divine Artist, has fashioned into the artwork of His creation.

Awaking Wonder at Home with Art

- Don't let the desire to do art "right" inadvertently take away your child's desire to do art at all. The first rule is, Let your child draw and color. Appreciate his art and encourage it; don't feel you need to correct it. Your child is communicating visually, so listen to him.

- There is no better way to help awaken wonder in your child toward God than by having her observe and draw nature. Encourage her to look for the fine details in God's creative artwork—in trees, clouds, mountains, and rabbits. God is in the wonder-full details of nature.

- Surround your children with real art that is beautiful and expressive—framed art, photography, carvings, stained glass, calligraphy. Keep art books on hand that can be casually enjoyed alone or together. And, of course, display your children's own artwork.

Wonder-full Words of God about Art

God saw all that He had made, and behold, it was very good. And there was evening and there was morning, the sixth day.

Genesis 1:31

Now the Lord spoke to Moses, saying, "See, I have called by name Bezalel, the son of Uri, the son of Hur, of the tribe of Judah. I have filled him with the Spirit of God in wisdom, in understanding, in knowledge, and in all kinds of craftsmanship, to make artistic designs for work in gold, in silver, and in bronze, and in the cutting of stones for settings, and in the carving of wood, that he may work in all kinds of craftsmanship."

Exodus 31:1–5

But now, O Lord, You are our Father, we are the clay, and You our potter; and all of us are the work of Your hand.

Isaiah 64:8

Finally, brothers, whatever is true, whatever is honorable, whatever is just, whatever is pure, whatever is lovely, whatever is commendable, if there is any excellence, if there is anything worthy of praise, think about these things.

Philippians 4:8 ESV

Wonder-full Ideas for Art

ACTIONS—What I can do

☐ _____

☐ _____

☐ _____

☐ _____

☐ _____

☐ _____

WORDS—What I can say

☐ _____

☐ _____

☐ _____

☐ _____

☐ _____

☐ _____

ENCOUNTERS—What I can arrange

☐ _____

☐ _____

☐ _____

☐ _____

☐ _____

☐ _____

RESOURCES—What I can acquire or provide

☐ *Educating the WholeHearted Child* by Clay and Sally Clarkson, chapter 13

☐ *Linnea in Monet's Garden* by Christina Björk, illustrated by Lena Anderson

☐ *Come Look with Me: Enjoying Art with Children* by Gladys S. Blizzard

☐ *A Child's Introduction to Art* by Heather Alexander, illustrated by Meredith Hamilton

☐ _____

☐ _____

☐ _____

10

Awaking Wonder through
WRITING

The SMART learning lens acronym owes its only phonetic aberration to the so-called "three Rs" of traditional education—Reading, 'Riting, and 'Rithmetic. We note the irony but are thankful for the slogan. It is one thing to read what others have written; it is something even more to write what others will read. The world has been shaped and changed by individuals who have written what entire civilizations have read and followed. The ultimate example, of course, is the Bible—the "sacred writings" that shape and guide us as Christians (see 2 Timothy 3:15–17).

Your children may not write things that change civilizations, but their writing might change ideas, people, plans, opinions, and even destinies. But only if you help your children see that good writing is not just knowing rules of mechanics and grammar, but also knowing how to use written words as a tool of their mind. Writing that will awaken wonder in your children is about using words powerfully, beautifully, clearly, persuasively, reasonably, personally. Words that can take many forms—essay, argument, poetry, fiction, narrative, history, testimony. Words that can touch many lives—family, friends, church, city, country, world.

The larger your child's vocabulary, and the wider his exposure to great ideas, the more his writing will become the means by which his mind will bring them all together. It is like driving a car rather than just owning one—driving opens new worlds to be explored in new ways. Writing is driving the mind into the world of words that can make ideas and imagination come alive in a permanent form. Writing incarnates verbally what is in the mind—it leads the mind into the wonder of the power and beauty of words, and of God, the Word of words.

Awaking Wonder at Home with Writing

- Good writing begins with reading and hearing good writing. Make sure your children read, and hear read aloud, the best age-appropriate stories, books, and poems in your home. Discuss with them why they like what they're reading and what makes it "good."

- Writing is time intensive and learned by doing. There is both skill and art to the kind of writing that will awaken wonder in a child for words as a tool for ideas and the imagination. Be intentional about creating writing time. Expect structure, but also allow for freedom.

- Make Write Nights part of your family culture. Gather your family together with your favorite writing tools, choose a topic for the night, and determine a set time for writing. Everyone shares, gives and gets feedback, edits, and rewrites. Save it all in a Write Night binder.

Wonder-full Words of God about Writing

For whatever was written in earlier times was written for our instruction, so that through perseverance and the encouragement of the Scriptures we might have hope.

Romans 15:4

"Therefore write the things which you have seen, and the things which are, and the things which will take place after these things."

Revelation 1:19

"Have you understood all these things?" They said to Him, "Yes." And Jesus said to them, "Therefore every scribe who has become a disciple of the kingdom of heaven is like a head of a household, who brings out of his treasure things new and old."

Matthew 13:51–52

In addition to being a wise man, the Preacher also taught the people knowledge; and he pondered, searched out and arranged many proverbs. The Preacher sought to find delightful words and to write words of truth correctly.

Ecclesiastes 12:9–10

Wonder-full Ideas for Writing

ACTIONS—What I can do

- [ ] _____
- [ ] _____
- [ ] _____
- [ ] _____
- [ ] _____
- [ ] _____

WORDS—What I can say

- [ ] _____
- [ ] _____
- [ ] _____

- [ ] _____
- [ ] _____
- [ ] _____

ENCOUNTERS—What I can arrange

- [ ] _____
- [ ] _____
- [ ] _____
- [ ] _____
- [ ] _____
- [ ] _____

RESOURCES—What I can acquire or provide

- [ ] *Educating the WholeHearted Child* by Clay and Sally Clarkson, chapter 11
- [ ] *Story Starters* by Karen Andreola
- [ ] *Poem Making* by Myra Cohn Livingston
- [ ] _____
- [ ] _____
- [ ] _____

11

Awaking Wonder through
TELLING

Talking is not the same as telling. As a FIRST learning priority, talk is about creating a verbal atmosphere at home that is rich with words. As a SMART learning priority, telling is about facilitating a narrative culture at home that is alive with dialog. It's a bit like breathing in and breathing out—inhaling words and exhaling thoughts, opinions, ideas, explanations, stories. But telling, unlike talk, is transitive—it requires a direct object. The best object of your child's telling is you, the parent.

The most basic form of telling for our children was the practice of narration—listening to a reading and "narrating" back what was heard. It was a simple learning exercise that encouraged attention, internalization, synthesis, and verbalization—all qualities of effective telling. The next step is telling without an artificial stimulus such as a reading. Telling is more than just conversing, though. It is dialoging with the goal of sharing with a listener what is in your own mind. Jesus was an effective and artful teller. His use of parable is a perfect example of telling—typically, His parables included a narrative story and an objective truth, and they were often told in a dialog with others. Jesus never wrote anything, but because He was an effective teller His words were heard, remembered, and written down by others.

Like with writing, it is in the process of telling that your children will be awakened to wonder about God. As they synthesize and verbalize to others ideas in their minds that are important to them, they will be shaping and sharpening their own stories and truths—awaking to new wonders of God's story and truth simply in the telling of their own. And in that process they will develop the ability to tell the wonder-full story and truth of the gospel, a telling that will become their testimony.

Awaking Wonder at Home with Telling

- Ask your children to tell you their stories—real or made up. Be prepared to offer story starters to prime the telling pump, to ask questions that will elicit more details, and to expect a satisfying conclusion that makes a point, a period (end), or a principle.
- Use the model of storytelling Sarah describes in her book *Caught Up in a Story* to teach your children a creative storytelling outline—exposition (set the stage), rising action (who, what, why), crisis (the turning point), falling action (decisions are made), and denouement (resolution).
- Model what good telling looks like and sounds like for your children through the art of storytelling. Tell your own life stories with lots of detail, drama, and pacing. Practice good telling by reading Bible stories that allow you to give voice to different biblical characters.

Wonder-full Words of God about Telling

While a large crowd was gathering and people were coming to Jesus from town after town, he told this parable: "A farmer went out to sow his seed."

Luke 8:4–5 NIV

"For God so loved the world, that He gave His only begotten Son, that whoever believes in Him shall not perish, but have eternal life."

John 3:16

"These commandments that I give you today are to be on your hearts. Impress them on your children. Talk about them when you sit at home and when you walk along the road, when you lie down and when you get up."

Deuteronomy 6:6–7 NIV

I will open my mouth with a parable; I will utter hidden things, things from of old—things we have heard and known, things our ancestors have told us. We will not hide them from their descendants; we will tell the next generation the praiseworthy deeds of the Lord, his power, and the wonders he has done.

Psalm 78:2–4 NIV

Wonder-full Ideas for Telling

ACTIONS—What I can do

☐ _____

☐ _____

☐ _____

☐ _____

☐ _____

☐ _____

WORDS—What I can say

☐ _____

☐ _____

☐ _____

- ☐ _____
- ☐ _____
- ☐ _____

ENCOUNTERS—What I can arrange

- ☐ _____
- ☐ _____
- ☐ _____
- ☐ _____
- ☐ _____
- ☐ _____

RESOURCES—What I can acquire or provide

- ☐ *Educating the WholeHearted Child* by Clay and Sally Clarkson, chapter 12
- ☐ *Journeys of Faithfulness* by Sarah Clarkson
- ☐ _____
- ☐ _____
- ☐ _____
- ☐ _____

REACH

LEARNING LENS

▼

Focus on Strength

RELATIONSHIPS
ENJOYMENTS
ABILITIES
CULTURE
HOME

REACH
Learning Lens
Focus on Strength

The Shema is arguably the most important passage of Scripture for the people of Israel (*shema* is the Hebrew word for "hear"). Devout Jews recite it daily: "Hear, O Israel: The Lord our God, the Lord is one. Love the Lord your God with all your heart and with all your soul and with all your strength" (Deuteronomy 6:4–5 NIV). In other words, the Israelites were to love God with all their being. Even "strength" in the passage is best understood as personal strength, not physical. It's about the force that makes one strong. It's about loving God with one's "muchness."

When Jesus repeats the words of the Shema in Greek, the term used is, again, about personal force (see Mark 12:30). We are to love God with absolutely everything that we are. Using the same word, Paul admonishes believers to "be strong in the Lord and in the strength of His *might*" (Ephesians 6:10, emphasis added). He is not saying we are to be physically strong like Jesus, but spiritually strong. The personal "might" that enabled Jesus to endure the cross is the same might that we have within us to love God—to love Him with all our spiritual strength.

Peter says we each receive a gift of grace from God to serve others and that we should serve "by the strength which God supplies" (1 Peter 4:11). The grace of God has shaped us to be who we are, but we have to express it. That's what we mean by *reach* in this section. We should always be reaching to become the person God made us to be. We're not provided personal strength just to be strong, but to reach our full expression as people so we can reach others by serving them.

When you awaken your children to the wonder of God's strength working within them, you are helping them become the unique and specially gifted people God has made them to be. But it's more. You are channeling that personal strength not just for your children's benefit, but also for the benefit of all those they will reach and serve for God.

When you focus on the REACH learning priorities in this section, you are helping your children to grow in the Lord's strength—to be strong in Him by becoming strong in the way He has made them to be. The more your children understand their own gifts and strengths, the more they will be able to use them, with God's strength, to serve others. That personal reach will give them the ability to reach the world God loves.

That kind of understanding doesn't come just from instructions and training, though—it comes mostly from modeling. Your children will become confident in who *they* are as they see that kind of confidence modeled in who *you* are. You awaken them to the wonder of how God can use them by being a mentor and model to them of your own reach.

— *Focusing My Life* —

As a mentor to my child, how am I focusing on my own strength? What am I doing to awaken wonder for God in my own personal life?

12

Awaking Wonder through
RELATIONSHIPS

Relationship is spiritual oxygen. We rarely think about inhaling and exhaling, but when we cease to breathe we cease to live physically. In the same way, we rarely think about loving and being loved, but when we cease to relate to others we cease to live spiritually. Relationship is part of the very fabric of creation—God created people to relate to Him, and to one another. The Trinity—Father, Son, and Holy Spirit—relate perfectly within the Godhead. Our ultimate destiny is to have eternal relationships with Jesus and His saints. Every page of Scripture, His loving conversation with us, is marked by relationship.

When Jesus was asked, "which is the great commandment in the Law?" His answer was relational—to love God, and to love your neighbor (see Matthew 22:35–39). This was acknowledged intellectually by other rabbis, but Jesus would show what that love looked like. He told His disciples, "Greater love has no one than this, that one lay down his life for his friends" (John 15:13). He would create a whole new "law," the law of love, that would replace the keeping of rules and regulations. Loving God and others would become the way that we please God, rather than keeping and enforcing rules.

Here's how this relates: If your children get lost in the dos and don'ts, or the doctrines and details, of Scripture, and they miss the big picture of what God wants to tell us and show us in His revelation to us of His heart, then they will miss the wonder of the gospel—that God loves them and wants to relate to them. Period. You can awaken them to that wonder only if they have experienced loving and being loved in their relationships with you, and only if you help them see the wonderful reality of relationship in the Word, in life, and in their own lives.

Awaking Wonder at Home with Relationships

- One of our best family traditions is the birthday breakfast. Everyone around the table tells the birthday child what makes her special or how she's grown, and we pray for her year ahead. It's relational practice not just for being loved, but also for loving others.
- Print out poster pages of your favorite Bible verses about relationships, family, and loving others. Use those verses for family devotional times, and talk about how they apply to everyday life. Put the verses on walls at child's eye level around the house.
- Have a ROAR morning—Reach Out And Relate. Have each child identify someone outside your home who needs to be helped, encouraged, or loved. Make a ROAR plan that includes both action and words—something special to do, and what your child can say to them.

Wonder-full Words of God about Relationships

"There is no greater love than to lay down one's life for one's friends. You are my friends if you do what I command."

John 15:13–14 NLT

Let us think of ways to motivate one another to acts of love and good works. And let us not neglect our meeting together, as some people do, but encourage one another, especially now that the day of his return is drawing near.

Hebrews 10:24–25 NLT

If I gave everything I have to the poor and even sacrificed my body, I could boast about it; but if I didn't love others, I would have gained nothing.

1 Corinthians 13:3 NLT

Therefore I, the prisoner of the Lord, implore you to walk in a manner worthy of the calling with which you have been called, with all humility and gentleness, with patience, showing tolerance for one another in love, being diligent to preserve the unity of the Spirit in the bond of peace.

Ephesians 4:1–3

Wonder-full Ideas for Relationships

ACTIONS—What I can do

☐ _____

☐ _____

☐ _____

☐ _____

☐ _____

☐ _____

WORDS—What I can say

☐ _____

☐ _____

☐ _____

☐ _____

☐ _____

☐ _____

ENCOUNTERS—What I can arrange

☐ _____

☐ _____

☐ _____

☐ _____

☐ _____

☐ _____

RESOURCES—What I can acquire or provide

☐ *Girls' Club* by Sarah, Sally, and Joy Clarkson

☐ *The Lifegiving Parent* by Clay and Sally Clarkson

☐ *Your Mom Walk with God* by Sally Clarkson

☐ _____

☐ _____

☐ _____

13

Awaking Wonder through
ENJOYMENTS

Every movie must distill big ideas into small scenes. The 1981 epic film *Chariots of Fire* told the story of Eric Liddell, the Scottish runner and 1924 Olympic gold medalist who died as a missionary in China. One moment in the movie beautifully captures the concept of enjoyments. When challenged by his sister for neglecting the work of God in China to run competitively, Eric tells her: "I believe that God made me for a purpose. For China. But He also made me fast, and when I run, I feel His pleasure. To give it up would be to hold Him in contempt."[1]

Perhaps there is no more important role you will play in your child's life than to awaken him to the wonder of the purpose for which God has made him—to give him freedom to enjoy the God-given messages and drives that not only will give him pleasure, but that will also bring honor to God. You can help your child uncover and discover what it is that will cause him to say as he matures into adulthood, "When I do that, I feel His pleasure." Those are the kinds of "enjoyments" this chapter is about—not worldly pleasures, but spiritual ones.

In the opening lines of the beautiful Psalm 139, David ponders the truth that God knows everything about him—his life, actions, thoughts, path, ways, and even words not yet spoken. He finally exclaims, "Such knowledge is too wonderful for me, too great for me to understand!" (Psalm 139:6 NLT). That kind of wonder comes only from knowing what God knows about you and knowing He has made you that way for His purpose and pleasure, and for your own. That is the wonder that you have the privilege as a parent to awaken in your child—the wonder and freedom of finding those enjoyments, God's purposes for them.

Awaking Wonder at Home with Enjoyments

- Create ACE messages for your children: Affirmation of what you see God doing in them ("I thank God . . ."); Confirmation of your heart for them ("I love . . ."); and Expectation of God's work in them ("I pray . . ."). They need to hear it from you. (Based on Philippians 1:3–11.)
- Take personal time with your child to imagine together how God might use her and what messages and desires He has put on her heart. If there is a developing enjoyment, consider what might help your child grow and develop in that area and provide that.
- As you begin to discern emerging spiritual messages, drives, and desires in your child (enjoyments), identify historical and contemporary figures who exemplify the same things. Find age-appropriate history books and biographies to read together with your child.

Wonder-full Words of God about Enjoyments

You go before me and follow me. You place your hand of blessing on my head. Such knowledge is too wonderful for me, too great for me to understand!

Psalm 139:5–6 NLT

Trust in the Lord with all your heart; do not depend on your own understanding. Seek his will in all you do, and he will show you which path to take.

Proverbs 3:5–6 NLT

Do not conform to the pattern of this world, but be transformed by the renewing of your mind. Then you will be able to test and approve what God's will is—his good, pleasing and perfect will.

Romans 12:2 NIV

I can do all things through Him who strengthens me.

Philippians 4:13

Trust in the Lord and do good; dwell in the land and enjoy safe pasture. Take delight in the Lord, and he will give you the desires of your heart.

Psalm 37:3–4 NIV

Wonder-full Ideas for Enjoyments

ACTIONS—What I can do

- ☐ _____
- ☐ _____
- ☐ _____
- ☐ _____
- ☐ _____
- ☐ _____

WORDS—What I can say

- ☐ _____

☐ _____

☐ _____

☐ _____

☐ _____

☐ _____

ENCOUNTERS—What I can arrange

☐ _____

☐ _____

☐ _____

☐ _____

☐ _____

☐ _____

RESOURCES—What I can acquire or provide

☐ *The Lifegiving Home* by Sally and Sarah Clarkson

☐ *Educating the WholeHearted Child* by Clay and Sally Clarkson

☐ *Culture Making: Recovering Our Creative Calling* by Andy Crouch

☐ COME LOOK WITH ME series (art for children)

☐ Albums by Classical Kids (classical music for children)

☐ _____

☐ _____

☐ _____

14

Awaking Wonder through ABILITIES

God does not wait until your children are grown and then suddenly drop gifts and skills into their lives that weren't there before. Long before any of our children approached their tweens, we could see their emerging abilities—Sarah, the future writer and thinker; Joel, the future musician and thinker; Nathan, the future creator and filmmaker; Joy, the future writer and influencer. We marveled at the developing interplay of their skills, gifts, and God-given personalities. Our children became as adults more of what they were as children.

As a parent, you have the incredible privilege and joy of shepherding your children into adulthood and giving them confidence to be the people God created them to be—to own their special abilities and gifts and to use them for God's purposes and to serve others. Perhaps it is significant that abilities is at the center of the REACH acronym. Your children's God-given skills, personality strengths, and gifts will be the fulcrum on which their self-understanding and their service to others will balance. They are reaching to become all God wants them to be.

James tells us that "every good thing given and every perfect gift is from above" (1:17). David exclaims, "Wonderful are Your works, and my soul knows it very well" because he is "fearfully and wonderfully made" (Psalm 139:14). And Jesus reminds us that God is a good Father who will "give what is good to those who ask Him" (Matthew 7:11). When you awaken your children to the wonder that God has crafted them and handmade them with a special purpose in mind—that their abilities are not just random things but God things—you awaken them to the realization that they have a special purpose in life to fulfill for God.

Awaking Wonder at Home with Abilities

- Watch for emerging skills and abilities in your children, and give them tools and opportunities to test them out—art, music, crafts, organization, sewing, building, design, cooking. Some will go away, but others will light a fire that you can continue to fan into flame.

- Keep in mind that personality is a kind of ability—it is an innate and God-given ability to think and see life skillfully from a particular perspective. Whatever personality inventory you use to understand your children, focus on the positive qualities that are their strengths.

- As obvious areas of special ability begin to develop in your child, gradually challenge him with new projects that use those skills, especially real-life opportunities. Also, find other trusted adults and tutors who can be examples and instructors of those abilities.

Wonder-full Words of God about Abilities

Every good and perfect gift is from above, coming down from the Father of the heavenly lights, who does not change like shifting shadows.

James 1:17 NIV

For you created my inmost being; you knit me together in my mother's womb. I praise you because I am fearfully and wonderfully made; your works are wonderful, I know that full well.

Psalm 139:13–14 NIV

"Which of you, if your son asks for bread, will give him a stone? Or if he asks for a fish, will give him a snake? If you, then, though you are evil, know how to give good gifts to your children, how much more will your Father in heaven give good gifts to those who ask him!"

Matthew 7:9–11 NIV

Each of you should use whatever gift you have received to serve others, as faithful stewards of God's grace in its various forms.

1 Peter 4:10 NIV

And whatever you do, whether in word or deed, do it all in the name of the Lord Jesus, giving thanks to God the Father through him.

Colossians 3:17 NIV

Wonder-full Ideas for Abilities

ACTIONS—What I can do

☐ _____

☐ _____

☐ _____

☐ _____

☐ _____

☐ _____

WORDS—What I can say

☐ _____

☐ _____

☐ _____

☐ _____

☐ _____

☐ _____

ENCOUNTERS—*What I can arrange*

☐ _____

☐ _____

☐ _____

☐ _____

☐ _____

☐ _____

RESOURCES—*What I can acquire or provide*

☐ *10 Gifts of Heart* by Sally Clarkson

☐ *Educating the WholeHearted Child* by Clay and Sally Clarkson, chapter 8

☐ *A Different Kind of Hero* by Sally and Joel Clarkson

☐ _____

☐ _____

☐ _____

15

Awaking Wonder through

CULTURE

Helping your children grow and reach for the best that God wants them to become means they will need to engage with culture. Wait, not that one—not the Culture with a capital C that we fear might somehow steal our children from us. Rather, culture with a small *c*. That kind of culture is two things: (1) It is the singular culture of art, music, and literature that, like a culture in a petri dish, grows a socially and intellectually enriched child; and (2) it is the many cultures in which they will live and bring life, like cultivating a garden with many kinds of plants—home, community, church, work, arts. Rather than just fearing Culture, help your children see themselves, in the words of Andy Crouch, as "culture makers" with a "call to faith" to create.[1] Awaken them to the wonder of culture making. To reach Culture, they need culture.

Your home is a microcosm of the two kinds of culture that your children will need. First, as you train your children's appetites to appreciate and desire the culture that comes from the fine arts, you are expanding their intellectual reach. They don't have to become fine artists, but they will have an internal standard for excellence in arts that will help them in every area of their lives. Second, your home culture is where they can freely experiment and explore what it means for them to be culture makers for God—to cultivate and bring life to a group of people with whom they live by being a faith-driven creative influence.

The apostle Paul recognized the reality of his reach into multiple cultures: "I have become all things to all people so that by all possible means I might save some" (1 Corinthians 9:22 NIV). Give your children that kind of reach as a faith-driven shaper of their cultures in life.

Awaking Wonder at Home with Culture

- Make enjoying the fine arts part of your home experience, not for mastery but simply for exposure and experience. Train the cultural appetites of your children with regular doses of good quality music, art, and literature. It will become a standard of excellence.

- Think of your home as a garden that you are keeping and cultivating. Family habits, routines, traditions, and rituals all create a special kind of culture in which your children will sink roots and grow. Think and plan carefully what kind of garden you are creating.

- Find ways that your children can be part of a community experience, not just as passive observers but also as active participants. Look for ways they can contribute art or music, offer a reading or performance, or just volunteer. Engage them in community culture.

Wonder-full Words of God about Culture

To the weak I became weak, to win the weak. I have become all things to all people so that by all possible means I might save some. I do all this for the sake of the gospel, that I may share in its blessings.

1 Corinthians 9:22–23 NIV

Do you see someone skilled in their work? They will serve before kings; they will not serve before officials of low rank.

Proverbs 22:29 NIV

Finally, brethren, whatever is true, whatever is honorable, whatever is right, whatever is pure, whatever is lovely, whatever is of good repute, if there is any excellence and if anything worthy of praise, dwell on these things.

Philippians 4:8

For we are God's handiwork, created in Christ Jesus to do good works, which God prepared in advance for us to do.

Ephesians 2:10 NIV

For the gifts and the calling of God are irrevocable.

Romans 11:29

Wonder-full Ideas for Culture

ACTIONS—What I can do

- ☐ _____
- ☐ _____
- ☐ _____
- ☐ _____
- ☐ _____
- ☐ _____

WORDS—What I can say

- ☐ _____
- ☐ _____
- ☐ _____
- ☐ _____

☐ _____

☐ _____

ENCOUNTERS—*What I can arrange*

☐ _____

☐ _____

☐ _____

☐ _____

☐ _____

☐ _____

RESOURCES—*What I can acquire or provide*

☐ *The Lifegiving Home* by Sally and Sarah Clarkson

☐ *The Lifegiving Table* by Sally Clarkson

☐ *Culture Making* by Andy Crouch

☐ _____

☐ _____

☐ _____

16

Awaking Wonder through
HOME

With the priority of home we come full circle from the very first learn-ing priority of faith. Together, they are a reminder that everything we've discussed has been about building a faith-shaped home—a Christian home. Hopefully by now one thing is clear: A Christian home is not defined by what the children are doing, but by what the parents are doing. Your children can consume all kinds of faith-based media, be involved in church clubs and Christian groups, and have only believing friends and still not live in a Christian home. As the mentoring parent, only you can make your home "Christian." In other words, it is not about having a "Christianized" home, but about making a home where Christ is living because His Spirit is alive in you. It is a Christ-alive home.

Home is where you are creating "good soil" in which your children can "hear the word in an honest and good heart, and hold it fast, and bear fruit with perseverance" (Luke 8:15). In that way, Jesus' parable of the sower is a picture of awaking wonder in your children—it is opening their hearts and minds to the living God who is alive and engaged personally in their lives through all that happens in your home. If you work to awaken them to the wonder of that reality, they will never be the same. They will be awaking to the wonder of God in all of life for all their lives, always reaching for all of God with all they are.

Home is the foundation for awaking wonder in your children. It is where you will grow all of the values, character, beliefs, convictions, confidences, and vision that will shape your children as future adults—their hearts, minds, and strengths. It is where their story with God will always find its beginning, and you are the one writing that story.

Awaking Wonder at Home with Home

- Prayer is putting faith into words and actions. It is an act of belief that God is alive, listening, and responsive. Make prayer a regular part of your home—family devotions, bedtimes, when needs arise, to thank God for blessings, and to worship Him with praise. Just pray it!

- Scripture is the source of the beliefs and values that will form the faith and spirituality of your child. Make Bible reading and discussion part of your home experience. We created *Our 24 Family Ways* for family devotions and training in biblical family values.

- Home is where your children's character and virtues will be trained and ingrained. It's not about enforcing rules and regulations, but about instilling habits and understanding—it's about living and learning together how to please God, others, and yourself.

Wonder-full Words of God about Home

But the seed in the good soil, these are the ones who have heard the word in an honest and good heart, and hold it fast, and bear fruit with perseverance.

Luke 8:15

These words, which I am commanding you today, shall be on your heart. You shall teach them diligently to your sons and shall talk of them when you sit in your house and when you walk by the way and when you lie down and when you rise up.

Deuteronomy 6:6–7

We will not hide them from their children. But we will tell the children-to-come the praises of the Lord, and of His power and the great things He has done. . . . Then they would put their trust in God and not forget the works of God. And they would keep His Law.

Psalm 78:4, 7 NLV

Fathers, do not exasperate your children; instead, bring them up in the training and instruction of the Lord.

Ephesians 6:4 NIV

Wonder-full Ideas for Home

ACTIONS—What I can do

☐ _____

☐ _____

☐ _____

☐ _____

☐ _____

☐ _____

WORDS—What I can say

☐ _____

☐ _____

☐ _____

☐ _____

☐ _____

☐ _____

ENCOUNTERS—What I can arrange

☐ _____

☐ _____

☐ _____

☐ _____

☐ _____

☐ _____

RESOURCES—What I can acquire or provide

☐ *The Lifegiving Home* by Sally and Sarah Clarkson

☐ *The Lifegiving Table* by Sally Clarkson

☐ *Every Moment Holy* by Douglas McKelvey

☐ _____

☐ _____

☐ _____

PLANNING

▼

A Twelve-Month Personal Planner

Personal Planner
Making a Wonder-full Home Life

Clay Clarkson

Clarksons plan. It's in our DNA. But we approach planning differently. As a relational idealist, Sally has a clear vision of where she wants to go and an internal itinerary of how she'll bring everyone with her to get there. As a logical realist, I also have a clear vision, but I map out the itinerary systematically in a way that makes the most sense to me to give everyone directions to follow. Different ways to plan, but both get us where we're going.

Sometimes the most difficult part of taking a trip or vacation can be the planning—making the itinerary. You know where you want to go, but you also know there are an endless number of ways you can choose to reach your destination. So you study the possible routes, read about stops along the way, highlight maps, calculate distances and times, and put it all in a binder, or an app, or a mental folder where it can help you keep the trip on track. But that itinerary can quickly become a source of stress when there is disagreement on choices, or guilt if things don't go as planned, or angst when you're faced with unforeseen detours and distractions. Despite the old axiom—"if you fail to plan, you plan to fail"—it seems more like the planning is failing.

This section of *The Awaking Wonder Experience* is where you'll do some actual planning for your journey to awaking wonder. It's where you'll make an itinerary for your family as you bring them along on the trip to the picture of what the Spirit has put in your heart. But rather than it being an onerous task that you fear will bring stress, guilt, and angst, we want your planning to be a positive and enjoyable task that leaves you feeling like you're headed in the right direction. Whether you are an idealist or a realist as a planner, we want you to feel like your planning is succeeding.

We don't want to push the metaphor too far, but this Twelve-Month Personal Planner is where the rubber meets the road. When we served in the discipleship ministry mentioned in chapter 1, a common axiom we learned about living by faith is that you can't steer a parked car—at some point you have to put your faith in gear and move onto the road. It's the same for your trip in the direction of this quality of family life we're calling awaking wonder. This chapter is where you can plan how to move forward in faith toward that kind of home life. And whether you "take it slow" or "get up to speed quickly" is up to you—there's not a right or a wrong way to move ahead by faith.

However, before you jump into your plan and hit the gas, we'd like to suggest some trip tips that can help you prepare the way for whatever ends up in your planning section. Remember that you're bringing your children along on a journey toward what the Spirit has put in *your* heart, but some simple groundwork will prepare *their* hearts to want to take that trip with you. You need to be intentional about it, but it won't take that much to get them excited about where you want to go. Here are just a few representative questions that will help you get them on board and keep them there.

Can you help me plan a new kind of trip? Invitation is the first step to participation. If you want your children to follow you on this journey to awaking wonder, it will begin with a positive invitation to capture their imaginations. Remember that it's not just about you. Do some parental vision casting, but make it about the reasons it will be fun, exciting, and meaningful for your children. It's really about them!

What else should we add to my AWEsome plans? Just for fun, you can call the Awaking Wonder Experience your AWEsome plan, and you can invite your children to offer their own AWEsome plans. The more they are involved in the actual planning of the plans you'll put in this section, the more they will buy in to the concept and practice of awaking wonder as a natural part of their lives.

What should we explore and talk about together? This kind of question should generate or stimulate lots of discussion and ideas. You will certainly hear some topics related to awaking wonder in their responses. Pick up on those and explore them further. Suggest some things you could do together based on some of the plans you've made. If you hear new good ideas, put those in your planner.

What snacks and treats should we plan to have? Food is spiritual. God made us to delight in the foods that He created for us to enjoy. A favorite and tasty snack or treat can add to the spiritual nature of the time you plan with your children no less than the things you read, hear, see, and talk about. "Taste and see that the Lord is good" (Psalm 34:8 NIV) is both metaphor and truth. Great tastes can awaken wonder to God.

What kind of music should we listen to together? There was a soundtrack to almost everything we did as a family—music that we all could enjoy, favorite musical artists, certain songs and albums. The right music can create a positive spiritual anchor in your child's spirit for your times together as a family. Give your children the privilege of choosing the soundtracks for the family times you plan.

May I tell you an interesting story about my childhood? Any story, any time, will always be of interest to your children. But stories about your own childhood memories that will reinforce what you are planning and suggesting for your family can be a kind of spiritual template. You can let your children know you want them to have those kinds of memories, too, and that's why you want to try to new things.

What does it mean to awaken wonder about God? Your children might surprise you with their answers to this more abstract question. Be sure to affirm their answers, and ask them questions that will encourage them to be even more specific. You can use this question in many different kinds of settings—at home, in nature, at a beautiful concert. It's about getting that language into their hearts and minds.

What do you think is wonderful about you? Children will not always know how to answer this question, but it will get them thinking and talking. Even better is that it will give you a way to talk about what *you* see that is wonderful in them—the ways God has made them, their unique skills or gifts, their character qualities. Help them see the wonder of who they might become as adults and how God can use them.

The most important thing about planning is not how much you do for each month—how many lines you fill in with things from the "Ideas" pages to say, to do, and to arrange—but just that you do some planning. Small steps will get you moving forward, and even a little work will work. Or, to restate the axiom about failing to plan with a more positive spin: If you plan your work, and work your plan, your plan will work.

With the exception of the "Resources" block for each month, the monthly planning pages are just lined without instructions. This is on purpose in order to give you maximum freedom to add whatever ideas you want in whatever way you want. The "Source" column is simply a way to notate what the idea is for and where it came from. So, for example, if it's a "Heart" idea from page 27, you can write "H/27" in that column space and then write out your idea (*H* for Heart, *M* for Mind, *S* for Strength). The rest is up to you, whether it's one great idea or ten.

You're set to go. Make some plans and start the journey of awaking wonder in your family. The God of wonder is waiting to join you.

TWELVE-MONTH
personal planner

JANUARY

Resources

FEBRUARY

Resources

MARCH

Resources

APRIL

Resources

MAY

Resources

JUNE

Resources

JULY

Resources

AUGUST

Resources

SEPTEMBER

Resources

OCTOBER

Resources

NOVEMBER

Resources

DECEMBER

Resources

Notes

Chapter 4: Awaking Wonder through Reading

1. Sarah Clarkson, *Read for the Heart: Whole Books for WholeHearted Families* (Anderson, IN: ApologiaPress, 2009), 26.

Chapter 5: Awaking Wonder through Story

1. Quoted in Andrew Peterson, "The Consolation of Doubt: An Address to the Buechner Institute," The Rabbit Room, August 31, 2016, https://rabbitroom.com/2016/08/the-consolation-of-doubt-an-address-to-the-buechner-institute/.

2. Sarah Clarkson, *Read for the Heart: Whole Books for Wholehearted Families* (Anderson, IN: ApologiaPress, 2009), 27.

Chapter 13: Awaking Wonder through Enjoyments

1. *Chariots of Fire*, directed by Hugh Hudson (1981; Burbank, CA: Warner Home Video, 2005), DVD.

Chapter 15: Awaking Wonder through Culture

1. Andy Crouch, *Culture Making: Recovering Our Creative Calling* (Downers Grove, IL: InterVarsity Press, 2008), 75 and 236.

About the Authors

Sally Clarkson is the mother of four wholehearted children, an inspirational conference speaker for more than twenty-five years, and a champion of biblical motherhood. She has inspired thousands of women through her *SallyClarkson.com* blog since 2007, and her *At Home with Sally* podcast has been downloaded millions of times. She also encourages women through her LifewithSally.com membership community and Mom Heart Ministry small groups. She is a bestselling author with over twenty books on motherhood, parenting, and Christian living, including *The Mission of Motherhood*, *Desperate* (with Sarah Mae), *Own Your Life*, *The Lifegiving Home* (with Sarah Clarkson), *Different* (with Nathan Clarkson), and *Mom Heart Moments*. Sally loves the companionship of her family, thoughtful books, beautiful music, regular tea times, candlelight, walking, and traveling to see her children.

Clay Clarkson is the executive director of Whole Heart Ministries, the non-profit Christian home and parenting ministry he and Sally founded in 1994. He has coordinated and overseen countless church workshops and over sixty ministry conferences. He has written or cowritten numerous books, including *Educating the WholeHearted Child*, *Our 24 Family Ways*, *Heartfelt Discipline*, and *The Lifegiving Parent*. He also conceives and writes books published by Whole Heart Press. Clay earned a master of divinity degree from Denver Seminary in 1985 and ministered on church staffs overseas and in the States before starting Whole Heart Ministries. He is also a songwriter and sometimes singer (you can find his music on PiecesofClay.com). After nineteen moves in three countries and four states, Colorado has been home for Clay and Sally since 2005 in Monument, in the shadow of Pikes Peak.

CLARKSON FAMILY

BOOKS & RESOURCES

Sally Clarkson

- *Seasons of a Mother's Heart*
- *The Mission of Motherhood*
- *The Ministry of Motherhood*
- *Dancing with My Heavenly Father*
- *Desperate* (with Sarah Mae)
- *You Are Loved* (with Angela Perritt)
- *10 Gifts of Heart*
- *Your Mom Walk with God*
- *Own Your Life*
- *The Lifegiving Home* (with Sarah Clarkson)
- *The Lifegiving Table*
- *Different* (with Nathan Clarkson)
- *Only You Can Be You* (with Nathan Clarkson)
- *Girls' Club* (with Joy and Sarah Clarkson)
- *Mom Heart Moments*

Clay Clarkson

- *Educating the WholeHearted Child* (with Sally Clarkson)
- *Our 24 Family Ways*
- *Heartfelt Discipline*
- *Taking Motherhood to Hearts* (with Sally Clarkson)
- *The Lifegiving Parent* (with Sally Clarkson)
- *The Lifegiving Parent Experience* (with Sally Clarkson)

Sarah Clarkson

- *Journeys of Faithfulness*
- *Read for the Heart*
- *Caught Up in a Story*
- *The Lifegiving Home* (with Sally Clarkson)
- *Book Girl*
- *Girls' Club* (with Sally and Joy Clarkson)

Joel Clarkson

- *The Lifegiving Home Experience* (with Sally Clarkson)
- *A Different Kind of Hero* (with Sally Clarkson)
- *The Lifegiving Table Experience* (with Sally and Joy Clarkson)

Nathan Clarkson

- *Different* (with Sally Clarkson)
- *Only You Can Be You* (with Sally Clarkson)
- *Good Man*

Joy Clarkson

- *Own Your Life Experience* (with Sally Clarkson)
- *The Lifegiving Table Experience* (with Sally and Joel Clarkson)
- *Girls' Club* (with Sally and Sarah Clarkson)

Sally Clarkson

AUTHOR | SPEAKER | LIFEGIVER

Beloved author and speaker Sally Clarkson has dedicated her life to mentoring and training women, encouraging mothers, and educating children. She has written more than twenty books on home, motherhood, homeschooling, and the Christian life. For daily encouragement and inspiration from Sally, you can find her online and on social media:

Website & Blog | SallyClarkson.com
Podcast Page | AtHomewithSally.com
Online Community | LifewithSally.com
Facebook | @TheRealSallyClarkson
Instagram | @Sally.Clarkson
Twitter | @Sally_Clarkson

Whole Heart Ministries

KEEPING FAITH IN THE FAMILY

Whole Heart Ministries is a nonprofit Christian home and parenting faith ministry founded by Clay and Sally Clarkson in 1994. Our mission is to give help and hope to Christian parents to raise wholehearted children for Christ, through ministries of writing, publishing, speaking, teaching, and training. For more information, visit us online and on social media:

Website & Store | WholeHeart.org
Facebook | @WholeHeart.org
Instagram | @WholeHeartMin